TOW TRUCKS
in Action

Larry Shapiro

MBI Publishing Company

First published in 1999 by MBI Publishing Company, PO Box 1, 729 Prospect Avenue, Osceola, WI 54020-0001 USA

MBI Publishing Company books are also available at discounts in bulk quantity for industrial or sales-promotional use. For details write to Special Sales Manager at Motorbooks International Wholesalers & Distributors, 729 Prospect Avenue, PO Box 1, Osceola, WI 54020-0001 USA.

Library of Congress Cataloging-in-Publication Data

Shapiro, Larry
    Tow trucks in action / Larry Shapiro
    p. cm.
    Includes index.
    ISBN 0-7603-0502-1 (pbk.)
    1. Wreckers (Vehicles) I. Title.
TL230.5.W74S53 1999
629.225--dc21   98-31989

On the front cover: After being involved in an accident with a car, this truck and its load went down a steep embankment. Ernie's Wrecker Service of Vernon Hills, Illinois, used a 1997 Century 9055 50-ton hydraulic wrecker on a Peterbilt 379 chassis and a 1984 Peterbilt 359 with a Challenger 50-ton hydraulic boom to extract the big rig. The steep embankment with a small creek at the bottom, combined with a snowy and slippery roadway, made for a challenging recovery.

On the frontispiece: Construction sites and roadwork often pose difficult and sometimes dangerous driving conditions. When a tanker slipped off this road, a mechanical wrecker with dual booms on a Kenworth chassis was used to pull it back onto level ground.

On the title page: A Freightliner tractor is hooked up to a heavy wrecker for the trip to the shop. The wrecker is a 1997 Mack Elite CL713 with a Century integrated hydraulic boom and under-lift.

On the back cover: Righting the truck was the easy part of this recovery for Oldenberg & Sons' Towing Company. Once the truck's owner pumped out the contents of corn oil into an empty tanker, Oldenberg righted this rig in about five minutes. They used a 1996 Kenworth T800 powered by a series 60 Detroit Diesel engine with a 70-ton DeWalt rotator. Also used in the recovery was a Kenworth unit with a Challenger hydraulic boom to steady the back end. After the tank truck was on its wheels, another Kenworth with a Century integrated hydraulic boom and under-lift was standing by to make the removal.

Edited by Anne T. McKenna
Designed by Dan Perry

Printed in Hong Kong

•CONTENTS•

•ACKNOWLEDGMENTS•

Writing any book requires tapping into many sources for information and help. This book was no different. Books, magazines, and trade literature are all valuable resources for raw information, but nothing can surpass the knowledge and assistance that I received from professionals who have spent their lives in this business. It is not uncommon to find second and third generations of families carrying on the traditions with the family name emblazoned on the side of their trucks. Sitting down with pen and notepad proved invaluable in gaining insight and learning about the trucks, the towing techniques, and the history involved in this industry. Although I believe that I have scarcely scratched the surface of this profession and its equipment, I am confident that the representation here will prove fulfilling for everyone who views this book.

As I met many people throughout the country who were willing to take the time to answer my naive questions, I learned about many areas of the towing business. Consolidation, safety, national standards, and motor club rates were among the hottest topics we discussed. But the most fun had to be working with the companies represented in the pages that follow. The true welcome that I received was phenomenal. Every company has thick volumes of photos showing the most remarkable incidents and recoveries. There was always a favorite job, a most hated job, and those run-of-the-mill jobs, which seemed pretty extraordinary to me.

I apologize to anyone who feels there are too many features from Illinois. Because I live there, I was able to be on the scene while the action was happening. I felt there was a need for the book to show what these fabulous trucks do every day, including the impressive recoveries. The biggest challenge that I had was in selecting the images. The incidents are so interesting that I thought many more shots should be included. This is where the expression "Behind every great man there is a great woman" comes into play. My wife Dorothy somehow mustered up the patience and tolerance to sift through all of the images and the stories in order to finalize the pages that follow. To her I owe my love and eternal thanks (and a vacation without tow trucks).

Many others contributed by providing their trucks and vast experience. In no particular order, I wish to thank the tow operators and company officials who put up with me. In Washington, Wayne Corey and Mike Smith with the United States Postal Service; also with the Post Office, Paul Snyder and Mike Wallace in Atlanta, and Green Davis in Chicago; in Massachusetts, Ed McCarthy and Patrick Esposito with MASSPIKE, and Frank Coady from Coady's Towing in Lawrence, a gentleman's gentleman who made sure my wife had plenty of hot coffee; in Maryland, Marv Wall and Richie with the MDTA, Wayne Sullivan of Sullivan's Garage in Baltimore, Dave Collette from Collete's Towing in Perryville, Jimmy Panos of Tart's Towing in Edgewood, and Mike Tauber of Tauber's Service in Linthicum Heights; in Indiana, Mike Oldenberg from Oldenberg and Sons in Hammond, along with Mark and Pug of Clover Leaf's Garage in Chesterton. Thanks to Carl Chase in Camp Douglas, Wisconsin, for finishing his multiyear project in time for pictures. In Illinois, I want to thank Marc Rogner of Rogner's Towing and Recovery in Palatine; John Picchietti of Pro Towing in Highland Park; J. R. Bramlett of Airline Towing in Calumet Park; Dan Murphy and his emergency crew at the CTA; Don Fenner of Northern Towing in Grayslake; Jack Allen of Allen's Corner Garage in Huntley; Pete Hallin and Jim Kissane of Jim's Towing in Bensenville; Ted Smith and the *Minute Men* of IDOT; Bill Parks of Transport Towing in Joliet; and a special thanks to Ernie Vole of Ernie's Wrecker Service in Vernon Hills.

As I work on a possible follow-up volume to *Tow Trucks in Action*, I look forward to working with more towing and recovery companies around the country to highlight their work.

Larry Shapiro

•INTRODUCTION•

Since their invention, trucks of all varieties have fascinated adults and children. Tow trucks are among the most interesting working trucks on the road today. Small, medium, and large trucks, in addition to flatbeds and specialized heavy wreckers, handle breakdowns, accidents, and unique recovery situations every day. This book is an introduction to these great trucks and concentrates on each type of tow truck as it does its job.

Chapter One covers the light-duty trucks which are the most visible because of their sheer numbers. Every town has a service station or mechanic who has at least one of these trucks. They are built on chassis similar to pickup trucks and can usually be spotted towing a disabled car.

Chapter Two discusses medium-duty trucks. These are slightly bigger and stronger than the light-duty trucks. The average person may not even notice the basic differences between the two, but the avid truck aficionado will spot them right away.

In Chapter Three, we see the heavy wreckers that haul big over-the-road tractor-trailers around with ease. When the big rigs break down, the heavy wreckers go to work. Each one has its own unique attributes and is customized to the needs of the operator who owns it. Great graphics and paint schemes make these trucks awesome to see.

Another type of tow truck is highlighted in Chapter Four. These are increasingly more common on the roads today. Most call them flatbeds, but the industry labels them carriers. In either case, they pull the disabled vehicle onto a flat deck for transport instead of lifting them by the front wheels like a regular tow truck. After reading this chapter, you will know why.

Probably the most interesting chapter is Chapter Five. It's amazing what kind of a mess big tractor-trailers can get themselves into. Great stories and real incidents illustrate the task of recovering trucks and cargo that end up in places they shouldn't be.

Although most tow trucks are owned by private companies, there are unique fleets around the country that are owned by the federal government, state governments, city, county, or local municipalities. Examples of these fleets are shown in Chapter Six with the specialized equipment that is often custom-made to handle unique assignments.

After examining this book, no one will ever be able to drive down the road again without suddenly noticing just how many tow trucks there are.

•ONE•
Light-Duty Trucks

The smallest tow trucks are the light-duty tow trucks. The different styles include wheel-lifts or those with hydraulic, mechanical, or fixed booms. Tow operators utilize changing technology to ensure safe transport of both old and new car designs. With this in mind, light-duty trucks can handle many situations, but they most commonly transport disabled vehicles. These tow trucks service motor clubs, independent garages, auto dealerships, and the general public. More specifically, they assist with vehicles that have flat tires, mechanical problems, overheated engines, dead batteries, or those that are stuck in the snow. It is easy to see why the United States alone has in excess of 38,000 towing companies.

The Trucks

The only tow truck that most people will ever come into contact with is the basic, small, light-duty tow truck from the local service station, roadside assistance service, body shop, or towing company. These units

When multiple cars are involved in an accident, a tow company needs to have several trucks available to clear the site. In this case it is extremely important, because a busy intersection is blocked.

Here is another multiple-vehicle accident where the towing company needed two units to clear the scene. A flatbed is used in addition to the light-duty truck.

that primarily tow cars or small trucks are the bread and butter of the industry. Far outnumbering the larger trucks, these units are virtually everywhere. They are built on a 1/2-ton or a one-ton chassis from one of Detroit's big three auto makers, most often on a Ford Super Duty or Chevy 3500-series chassis. These are known as Class III & IV chassis with gross vehicle weights (GVW) from 10,000 to 16,000 pounds and engines between 195 and 300 horsepower.

The trucks feature bodies and booms built by major companies like Holmes,

Jerr-Dan, Signature Series, Vulcan, Chevron, No-Mar, Eagle, AATAC, Century, or Challenger, or have home-made bodies and boom assemblies built by the operators themselves. Some have the newest technology, fancy paint schemes, and rows of running lights, while others might be on their second- or third-generation owners with plenty of body rust, many road miles behind them, and no end in sight. It is not uncommon to find tow truck odometers reading well in excess of 100,000 miles. Since some companies relish the newest equipment, they will continually replace their trucks, selling the older ones to other companies not desiring brand-new units.

Towing Equipment

Towing manufacturers, as in any other industry, continue to provide new equipment designs and technology for ease of operation and increased safety for both the operators and the owners of the vehicles being towed. The trucks also have to be able to keep up with the towing requirements for new car designs. Light-duty tow trucks generally have lifting capacities from 4,000 to 16,000 pounds.

Fifteen years ago, the norm for all light-duty tow trucks was either a fixed, welded pipe boom or a mechanical boom assembly. Pipe booms are simply an arrangement of large-diameter steel pipes welded together usually in an "A" configuration to hold the cables that attach to the car. More sophisticated mechanical booms can swivel and have some vertical movement.

Attached to the end of the boom was a chain hookup, bar-type hookup, or harness assembly for towing a car. A chain hookup is merely a set of chains used to secure parts of the car's front axle to the rear of the tow truck. The bar-type assembly attaches chains to a steel bar at the base of the boom.

The harness, which is also known as a sling, was introduced in the 1950s. It is a rectangular piece of equipment with steel bars

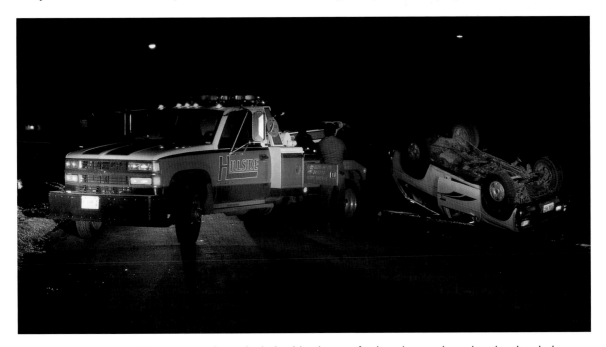

The teenage driver of this sport utility vehicle had his license for less than a day when he decided to show his friends how stunt drivers are able to make a U-turn while backing down the road without stopping. After he flipped his parents' new car, this Chevy C30 with a hydraulic boom was used to winch the car right side up.

Sometimes even tow companies need a lift. Here a Ford F350 with a Vulcan boom pulls a sister truck after a slight mishap.

on the top and bottom. Large strips of thick rubber on the sides act as a cushion protecting the front of the car from the steel pieces. Most bumpers at that time were heavy steel, and the rubber pieces known as sling straps prevented scratching.

Although this method is still in use today and is a feature available on most brand-new units, the booms are no longer mechanical. Whether a sling or bar is used, each is attached to a steel cable, which runs along the boom to a winch. Modern tow trucks are made with hydraulic booms. Instead of relying on gears, hydraulic cylinders are the backbone of these vehicles.

Several years ago, a new design was introduced in an attempt to keep any type of sling or harness from touching the front of the vehicle. Although its popularity was not long-lived, this design featured a wide steel bar attached to the top of the boom, which

extended the width of the tow truck. Attached to either end of the bar were special straps hanging down and connecting to another assembly that wrapped around each of the front wheels. Called the Cradle Snatcher II by the Vulcan Company, this design offered towing without touching the front bumper area at all.

Wheel-lifts

As time went on, new car designs, sport utility vehicles, and plastic bumpers required manufacturers to devise a new way to tow vehicles damage-free. Wheel-lifts were introduced as the next generation of towing techniques. Generally, although not exclusively, a wheel-lift is incorporated into a truck with a conventional boom and winch.

Using wheel-lifts, tow trucks operate a separate device at the base of the truck, which lowers to the ground and extends under the bumper to the front wheels of the disabled vehicle. Then, a steel section called an L-arm is placed behind each tire and attached to the wheel-lift assembly. This locks the tires into the wheel-lift, allowing the car to be raised by the tires and axle without anything touching the front of the car.

Wheel-lifts provide for quick, simple, and damage-free towing. They are also handy for a car that has front-end damage that makes it difficult to hook up. Typically, this is how a car will be towed from an accident scene.

Sometimes, a car needs to be towed when it is parallel-parked between other

Here is an example of a conventional wheel-lift with L-arms that attach around the outside of the tires.

A wheel-lift is out of the question since the front tires were burned away by fire. The car must be towed using the sling. Additional damage to the front end is not a big concern here.

A local tow company, with a police contract for accident removal, hooks one car while another waits its turn in the center of a busy intersection during rush hour.

vehicles. As a result, another wheel-lift design came forth. The newer system makes this task easy and can be manipulated without requiring the operator to leave the cab of the truck. The tow truck can be set perpendicular to the parked car, push the wheel-lift underneath, and set the tire restraints by remote. Since curbs can hamper access around the tires, these newer units pivot from between the tires where there is plenty of unobstructed space.

Several companies market self-loading wheel-lifts with a claw system that literally grips the tires when they come into contact. Hookups can be achieved in seconds instead of minutes. These wheel-lifts, perfect for the city or private towing companies, grab your car when you park it in the wrong place just for a few minutes.

Not all tow trucks have special bodies built around the booms. A tow operator who wishes to spend less money on a truck can purchase a standard pickup truck and place a removable boom assembly into the truck's bed. Resting on a small frame, the boom can be removed quickly to allow the truck to be used as a conventional pickup.

All tow trucks incorporate a winch. Winches are used to draw a vehicle toward the truck to secure for towing, bring vehicles back onto their wheels, or rescue a vehicle that is stuck somewhere off the road. The winch has a cable that runs along the boom assembly to the rear of the truck. Additional winches can also be mounted on the front bumper or in the bed of the truck separate from the boom.

Assisting a motorist who locked herself out of her van is a routine service call for many local towing companies. This truck features an Isuzu chassis.

Here is an example of a standard pickup truck with a towing unit in the bed. The boom setup can be removed from the bed in a matter of minutes, allowing the truck to have more than one identity. In addition to towing a vehicle, the truck can be used for hauling and moving, like any other pickup truck on the road.

15

It is more common than one might think to find cars that need to be set up on their wheels following a collision. Here an operator flips a late model Buick using a homemade mechanical boom assembly on a Ford chassis.

The Jobs

Most of the duties associated with light-duty tow trucks center around roadside assistance and moving disabled vehicles for service. In addition to these routine tow jobs, light-duty tow trucks respond to remove vehicles from accident scenes. Whether the vehicle is blocking traffic or not, if it is unable to move under its own power, it will be towed.

Once the damaged cars are removed from the roadway, the tow operator's job is not yet complete. It is the operator's responsibility to clean up and remove all broken parts from the car including glass and any debris in the roadway. Although the operator

may be asked to drop a small amount of sand on a slippery spot, it is a fire department's responsibility to wash down any large quantities of liquids such as gas, oil, or transmission fluid that may create a hazard. Along with tools and chains, the tow truck will store a broom, shovel, and usually an empty five-gallon plastic can for garbage.

At an accident scene, tow operators need to be concerned for their own safety from passing motorists. Everyone has driven by an accident scene wanting to see just what has happened. Sometimes, drivers who are looking at the wreck cause a second accident or fender bender because they aren't keeping their eyes on the road.

This is yet another instance where a sport utility vehicle winds up in an unnatural position. Both of the occupants were thrown from the vehicle and, tragically, one was killed. Police, fire, and highway officials work at the scene as the tow operator prepares to bring the vehicle upright.

Occasionally, a tow operator will be injured by one of these drivers. Fortunately, accidents of this nature are rare.

These days, it is not unusual to find a car or sport utility vehicle on its side or upside down. This can result from a collision with another vehicle, or it can occur when the driver has left the road and traveled down an embankment. In addition, flipping a vehicle may be due to the displaced center of gravity found in many sport utility vehicles. Many drivers are unfamiliar with how little it takes to turn some of these vehicles on their sides, and tow operators are routinely finding them in very awkward positions.

Tow trucks perform vital functions that keep cars running, lanes open, and motorists on their way. Light-duty tow trucks, an important part of the complete towing industry, provide a vital community service.

Two small, homemade trucks on Ford chassis clear a head-on collision while the fire department stands by to wash the transmission fluid from the roadway.

·TWO·
Medium-Duty Trucks

Medium-duty tow trucks are a little bigger than the light-duty trucks. As the weight and size of the chassis grows, so does the ability to increase the payload that it carries. This is true whether the truck is used for moving, making deliveries, dumping, or towing. As the class of the chassis increases, the wrecker boom and body grow. Consequently, so does the size of the vehicle it can tow. Due to their size, these trucks do everything that the light-duty units can and more.

The Trucks

Some medium-duty chassis are made by Detroit's big three auto makers, but the industry is dominated by companies specializing in the building of trucks. Names like Navistar (IHC), Freightliner, Mack, and Volvo join Ford and General Motors in supplying this segment of the market. Chassis most common in this class are the IHC 4000 series and the Freightliner Business Class series, with engines ranging from 200 to 400 horsepower. The GVW range begins where the light-duty trucks leave off and is

When a tractor-trailer overturned with coils of banded steel inside, a medium-duty unit was used to remove the coils from the trailer.

19

A shuttle of two medium-duty Vulcan hydraulic units, one with a Ford F800 chassis and the other on a Chevy C6500 chassis, are used to off-load an overturned tractor-trailer carrying coils of steel bands. Each unit takes turns backing the load up onto a lowboy until the job is complete. Total time for the recovery was about three hours.

between 18,000 and 35,000 pounds. These trucks are considered Class V - VII, sit higher than the light-duty trucks, and have greater visibility–a factor some drivers prefer.

Booms and bodies for these units are manufactured by the same companies that build the light-duty trucks, and the technology and designs are also the same. The main difference is that in proportion to the heavier chassis, the towing and lifting capacities are increased over their smaller cousins. Generally in the 10- to 20-ton range, medium-duty rigs can lift twice the capacity of some light-duty units.

Winches

One constant for every tow truck today is a winch. In fact, it is not unusual to see more than one winch mounted on a truck. Basically, a winch is a motor, some cable, and a drum. Cable is wound around the drum and is let out to hook up to a vehicle or other item needing to be moved. After being attached, the motor reverses the direction of the drum and draws the cable in. Winches have different capacities ranging from 1,000 to 100,000 pounds. The diameter of the cable itself can be anywhere from 1/4 of an inch to 1 1/2 inches for special applications.

Depending on the power system of the truck, the winch can be either electric or

A medium-duty Vulcan unit on a Chevy C6500 chassis is used to upright a tractor-trailer whose load shifted while rounding a highway entrance ramp too quickly.

hydraulic, and one of two types. The first type is called a worm gear. This winch is rated based on the number of times the cable is wrapped around the drum. The more cable that is on the drum, the lower the capacity of the winch. The second type is called a planetary. A planetary winch is stronger and more costly than a worm gear. This is the choice for most heavy recovery work, since planetary winches maintain the same rating regardless of the number of times the cable is wrapped around the drum.

The Jobs

A general rule of thumb for towing is that you cannot tow anything that is heavier than the tow truck itself. This creates a niche for the medium-duty tow trucks. Since medium-duty trucks have become very popular with delivery companies, utility companies,

Before the hydraulic units being built today were available, mechanical units like this 1986 Holmes 600 were the norm. Many are still in active service.

Here is an example of a bar-type hookup being used on this truck that rolled over. The tow truck is a Freightliner FL60 with a Signature Series back end.

A uniquely colored Holmes 600 dual-boom mechanical wrecker with an array of brightly color-coded chains.

and construction companies, breakdowns of these vehicles require towing by medium-duty tow trucks.

Similar to the light-duty trucks in every way except size and lifting capacity, the medium-duty units provide added opportunities to the tow company. They will respond to accident scenes, routine tows, and roadside assistance. If the tow company is not sure what they will encounter when they respond to a call for help, perhaps the medium-duty unit will be sent with its expanded capabilities instead of a light-duty truck. The big rigs, however, can do even more.

•THREE•
Heavy Wreckers

The big rigs aren't called tow trucks. They are known as heavy wreckers! Many appear the same, but in reality they offer quite a few differences. Modern heavy wreckers can feature rotators, separate hydraulic booms with under-lifts, or an integrated boom and underlift. Older models have mechanical booms, and those that are homemade can feature a combination of customized options. These sit on Class VIII chassis with single, dual, or triple rear axles and have lifting capacities ranging from 26,000 to upwards of 120,000 pounds. Total GVW can top 72,000 pounds or 36 tons.

The Truck Cab and Chassis

Any conventional heavy truck chassis can provide the base for a heavy wrecker, and all of the major truck companies may be spotted in some operator's fleet. Most common among the major U.S. towing and

When a fully loaded cement mixer breaks down, it is important for the material company to off-load the ready-mix before removing the truck. The 1989 Mack Super Liner featured here is powered by an E7 400 Mack engine with a Challenger 8088 50-ton hydraulic boom. It has a separate hydraulic system to power the cement mixer so that it can run normally to empty its drum before being towed away.

It may not look like much is left of this tractor, but the tow operator needs to be able to hook up the remains and safely tow this demolished tractor-trailer to the yard. The wrecker has a 1974 Hendrickson chassis and features a Holmes 750 wrecker with dual mechanical booms. (To see the remains of the cab, refer to Chapter Four.)

recovery companies, though, are Peterbilt, Mack, Freightliner, and Kenworth. The most popular Peterbilt chassis include the 357, 376, and 377 models, while the most popular Kenworth chassis include the T600B, T800B, and W900B. This book also features wreckers with chassis from White-Volvo, Diamond REO, Oshkosh, International Harvester (IHC), Hendrickson, and Autocar. Basic requirements for chassis include minimum Resisting Bending Moment (RBM) for each frame rail from 1,000,000 to 4,000,000 inch-pounds. Integral strength is imperative to prevent damage to the recovery vehicle.

Wreckers may have sleeper compartments behind the cab. Operators who do long-haul towing require a sleeper so the driver can stop and rest comfortably at truck stops. Others use the sleeper compartment to store a change of clothing, tools, or perhaps a cooler with supplies for a prolonged job. The sleeper also offers the opportunity to relax or nap while waiting to go to work at some of the more drawn-out recoveries. It is not uncommon to wait 4 to 10 hours while hazardous product is drained from a tanker before the tow operator gets the go-ahead to start working.

Mechanical Wreckers

Years ago, all heavy wreckers were mechanical. The booms were in a fixed position while towing. They had a system of gears, pulleys, and cables for towing and winching. Some trucks had dual booms with the ability to swivel over the side of the truck's body. Companies like Holmes and

The other truck involved with the demolished tractor is this R Model Mack tandem dump truck. The heavy wrecker is a 1980 Hendrickson with a homemade boom and body.

Weld-Built were known for this type of design. Although some of the booms had the capability to be extended, this had to be done manually before any load was placed on the cables. The boom could also be raised or lowered. This too was done by hand and needed to be done before any weight was carried on the cables. An operator could expect an hour's work to make any height and extension adjustments. Many of these units are still in full operation today, and as the units wear, the gears need adjustment to permit steady and consistent pulling.

Hydraulic Wreckers

In the late 1960s and early 1970s, the next generation of wrecker was introduced with hydraulic cylinders, creating a single, heavier, stronger boom. Although these units have more moving parts and require more maintenance than the mechanical units, the benefits are worth the added costs. The boom can be raised, lowered, and extended so the operator has more options for towing and recovery work. Unlike the mechanical booms, hydraulic booms can be raised, lowered, extended, and retracted with the load attached. The capacity of the booms varies by style and is rated differently based on the angle of elevation and how far it extends past the truck.

Certain conditions require a load to be lifted very far off the ground. Hydraulic booms offer the operator the ability to raise the boom high in the air to allow sufficient clearance in these situations. Mechanical

This 1987 Kenworth T800 has a 3406 Caterpillar engine, 13-speed transmission, and a 1992 40-ton NRC Mid-Slider. Fitted to the under-lift is a conventional wheel-lift assembly for trucks. Some tow operators prefer wheel-lifts to under-lifts for simplicity of the hookup, because they are quick and easy. Some tractors have oil pans that hang low and can interfere with under-lift units. Wheel-lifts are the answer for these trucks.

and pipe booms are limited in their capacity to provide the height needed for lifting an object off the ground.

Today, hydraulic wreckers come in four basic varieties: separate boom and under-lift, integrated unit, under-lifts, and rotators.

Separate Boom and Under-lift

One version offers a conventional boom and may have a separate under-lift unit mounted at the rear of the truck. Unlike smaller units that use wheel-lifts, the under-lift reaches under the truck's cab and lifts from the axle. The boom and under-lift function independently of one another. In order to use the boom, the under-lift unit is folded down out of the way. One drawback to this style of truck is the limit to which the under-lift can be raised into the air.

Integrated Unit

The second style is referred to as an integrated unit. With this unit, the under-lift is attached to the boom and they function together. This unit allows the operator a bit of additional freedom of movement to lift a

A custom-made under-lift unit supports a disabled tractor.

truck higher off the ground. It also offers greater lifting capacities with the under-lift, since it is part of the boom. Some operators prefer the integrated unit because it offers superior weight distribution for the load being carried. Since the under-lift is attached to the boom, and the boom is mounted in the center of the truck, the weight at the rear is distributed over the entire chassis. In contrast, when a truck has a boom with a separate under-lift, it is attached to the rear of the truck chassis. This means the under-lift bears all the weight of a tow on the rear of the wrecker.

Under-lifts

The third type of hydraulic unit simply utilizes an under-lift for truck towing and winching. Since this unit lacks a boom, it is mainly used to move disabled trucks. Although these units still have tremendous winching power, generally, a unit with a boom will be sent to the recovery jobs because of its added capabilities.

Under-lifts can be fitted with accessories to make them into wheel-lifts. Working on the same principle as smaller tow trucks, the wheel-lift is secured around the front or rear wheels of the truck and locked into place. Special wheel restraints are used to secure the wheels into the wheel-lift assembly for safety. These are made of a tough nylon material and are pulled tight using a ratchet system.

Tow operators who use wheel-lifts instead of under-lifts feel this is an easier and quicker hookup. The driver does not have to crawl under the disabled truck, which can be filthy.

When this tanker overturned, the tanks ruptured and the hazardous cargo began to leak. With fire department teams standing by, another tanker was brought in to pump the cargo out of the damaged rig. The 1988 Peterbilt Century 1040 heavy wrecker then righted the tanker and towed it away. Total time from the accident until the ramps were opened was 11 hours.

Another reason to use the wheel-lift is that some large trucks have an oil pan that hangs very low in the front. Using the under-lift assembly would risk damaging the oil pan, whereas the wheel-lift is nowhere near it.

One down side to the wheel-lift is the length that it adds to the wrecker and the amount of work necessary to remove the assembly if it is physically in the way for recovery work. Generally, heavy wheel-lifts will be a part of a wrecker whose primary function is towing disabled trucks and not recovery work.

Rotators

The fourth type of hydraulic unit is known as a rotator. Rotators are the biggest, most expensive, and most versatile of the heavy wreckers. They have a hydraulic boom capable of lifting between 35,000 and 120,000 pounds, depending on the distance the boom is extended from the truck. They can rotate up to a full 360 degrees around the truck body to facilitate recovery operations. Rotators allow the operator to position the truck to work off one side and still swivel the load around the truck to safely place it elsewhere.

When the rotator is set up, outriggers or stabilizers just behind the cab section will come out like giant legs. The rear of the wrecker will have either an outrigger, a spade, or a downrigger which simply extends straight down for stabilization. A rotator boom can extend up to 15 feet beyond the wrecker itself.

A routine tow for a truck requires disconnecting the drive shaft to protect the transmission. This 1990 IHC with a Vulcan 45-ton integrated boom and under-lift is used to tow a tractor that won't start. When it was not possible to disconnect the driveshaft, the tow operator had to disconnect the axles before towing.

Rotators are often the pride of a fleet. Unquestionably the most expensive recovery vehicle, it is also the biggest. Today, these units new cost upwards of $300,000. That's no small investment. Companies that buy rotators are involved in serious recovery work and often find the need to refine these units to suit their individual needs.

The Job

Any run-of-the-mill breakdown requiring a wrecker to tow a large truck is no simple one, two, three, hookup. Unlike a car, which can be hooked and snatched in as little as two to three minutes, a truck requires more work. Although the truck can be towed short distances without any major modifications, before any serious towing is done the operator must first decide whether to tow from the front or the rear. If there is a trailer involved, the answer is obvious. A tractor by itself, however, offers either option.

When towing from the front, the tow operator needs to disconnect the drive shaft to avoid ruining the transmission. If the truck should slip into gear en route to the

It doesn't matter how big a truck is. Any contest involving a train always goes to the train. The driver of this dump truck did not survive this encounter. Witnesses claim he went around the crossing gates after they were down. A Century heavy wrecker with an integrated boom and under-lift was used to remove the remains of the tractor. The rear tandems and the fifth wheel from the tractor stayed with the dump trailer.

garage, the teeth on the gears would be completely stripped. If the drive shaft is corroded or otherwise prevents the tow operator from disconnecting it on the road, it then becomes necessary to disconnect the axles. Trucks that are a year old are fairly straightforward to work on because everything comes apart easily. Trucks that are several years old, though, can be more difficult because of corrosion, road grime, and wear that hampers removal of nuts and bolts. This process can take up to two hours. Adverse weather conditions such as subzero temperatures or blowing rain or snow can extend this time frame.

If the decision is made to tow from the rear, no axle or drive shaft modification is required. One concern, though, is whether or not the truck has a turbo engine. If it does, then the vertical exhaust pipes need to be covered to prevent air from being pushed into the engine and burning up the turbo. Another concern is with the wind deflectors that some tractors have installed on the roof. Since a deflector is designed for forward motion, pulling it backwards can risk damaging the deflector if it is not properly secured.

Some wreckers can be operated by a hard-wired remote control box. This allows the operator to maneuver all of the controls from an area that provides optimal safety or a better vantage point. On a basic towing job, this can save quite a bit of time walking back and forth unnecessarily making small adjustments to get under the rig to disconnect the drive shaft.

At a major accident scene, the police and highway agencies (and the motoring public) prefer rotators for recovery work because they permit the operator to work off the side of the truck, minimizing the amount of lane blockage or roadway to be shut down. A conventional wrecker would need to block several lanes in order to work off the back of the rig. The authorities want to open as many lanes of traffic as possible, after ensuring the safety of emergency personnel, including the recovery crew. In today's environment, the ideal scenario preferred by everyone is to keep the traffic flowing.

Some recovery operations can take several hours, so having the right equipment for the job is a must. Most states have specific requirements, including access to a rotator or a crane, for companies to be able to do recovery work on major highways.

Unique Rigs

One unique rotator belongs to Airline Towing, Inc., on Chicago's South Side. An authorized recovery company for many

With the train looming in the background, the dump trailer can be seen with the tractor's rear axle still attached.

After a two-year ordeal to secure an M60 tank for the local VFW Lodge, the tank arrived and was unloaded in the parking lot. When it came time to move it to a concrete slab for display, the lodge called for help. Three heavy wreckers were needed to turn the 60-ton tank before winching it into place. The wreckers that were used included a 1985 45-ton NRC wrecker on a Freightliner chassis, a 1997 Challenger wrecker on a 1991 IHC chassis, and an NRC 45-ton Sliding Rotator on a Peterbilt 376 chassis.

Chicago area highways and tollways, Airline claims to have the largest rotator in the country. Unit #444 has a 1996 tri-axle Kenworth T600 chassis with a 400-horsepower Cummins engine. It has an overall length of 48 1/2 feet with a 60-ton Challenger wrecker body and boom. This unit was designed to provide a broader working platform and allow superior stabilization to handle loads off the back end.

A Canadian company called NRC builds wreckers with a different twist. Actually it's not a twist at all, but a slide. Called Sliders, these units have the capability for the entire boom mechanism to slide 10 feet back and forth in the body of the truck. Since a boom's maximum lifting capacity is achieved without any extension, this provides a 10-foot area behind the wrecker where the operator can utilize this full potential. As long as the operator can properly anchor the front end, the slider gives more lifting power at each point along the 10-foot range.

These units are available with different ratings between 20 and 60 tons and the sliding boom can also be incorporated into a rotator. The rotators feature under-body horizontal stabilizers that raise the entire wrecker off the ground. While in use, the operator can make adjustments to the wrecker's position from side to side without shutting down. This can be particularly useful when setting up near the edge of the pavement. The setback made necessary by the stabilizers can be reduced while maintaining the firm footing required for safety.

Although rotator is a name the towing industry gives to a heavy wrecker with up to 360 degrees of continuous boom rotation, these capabilities are not limited to rotators. Some towing and recovery companies supplement or replace these units with a conventional crane that is commonly associated with the construction industry.

In the northwest suburbs of Chicago, Ernie's Wrecker Service, Inc., sold their 70-ton tri-axle All Pro rotator and replaced it with a construction-grade #1550 National Crane. Mounted on a 1997 Peterbilt 357 chassis, this unit is powered by a 375-horsepower Caterpillar engine through a 13-speed transmission. Unlike rotators, the crane features an enclosed operators' cab on the turntable at the base of the crane's boom. Instead of standing at the back of the truck, the operator rotates with the boom for a better vantage of the recovery being performed. This unit has dual rear axles and a GVW of 53,000 pounds. The crane's capacity is 36 tons with the ability to reach 103 feet and rotate 360 degrees.

Camp Douglas, Wisconsin, is the home of a giant wrecker. In fact, this just might be the biggest wrecker ever made. Built for serious recovery work in the shops of Carl L. Chase, this custom unit was in production for over 10 years. Sitting on a Peterbilt 359 chassis, the overall length is 40 feet. The

Arguably the largest heavy wrecker ever built, this five-axle Peterbilt has a 100-ton hydraulic boom that can extend over 100 feet.

truck has five axles, a KTA 600-horsepower Cummins engine, and two Spicer transmissions with 40 forward gears. The first transmission is a five-speed and the auxiliary is an air shift with a four-speed overdrive. Two 100,000-pound winches run 800 feet of 1 1/2-inch cable with the capability for massive winching. The four-section boom can lift 100-plus tons and can extend over 100 feet.

Heavy wreckers provide the towing industry with the greatest power for the biggest jobs. Each unit may look or function differently, but they all share the largest capacities for towing, winching, and lifting. Whether the unit is mechanical or hydraulic, in the hands of the skilled operators, the job gets done.

•FOUR•
Carriers

Another common sight on the road today is a different type of tow truck. Actually, in the trade it is not referred to as a tow truck at all. This truck is distinctively different from the light-, medium-, and heavy-duty trucks featured in the previous chapters, while at the same time it shares certain characteristics. Commonly referred to as a flatbed, it is also known as a car carrier, carrier, or roll-back. What these units have in common with tow trucks is a winch, usually a wheel-lift at the rear, and the mere fact that they are used to transport cars and trucks from one point to another.

Carriers came into being in the late 1970s and early 1980s because of changing trends in automotive aerodynamics and design. Many vehicles could not be towed damage-free with sling-type equipment. Carriers were designed to tow vehicles in a level position on a flat bed made of aluminum or steel. These units can tow up to four vehicles at a time, depending on the carrier's design.

Called The Right Approach by the manufacturer, a new carrier design features an end section that will lie almost flat on the ground for towing cars that have very little ground clearance. This unit is ideal to provide the special care required for a 1988 slant-nose Porsche 911 Turbo S sports car. The truck is a 1997 IHC 4700 with a Century carrier.

H ere is a close-up showing the hinged rear deck section loading a sports car with minimal ground clearance.

Loading and Unloading

The basic principle of operation is simple and straightforward. The carrier backs up to the disabled vehicle, leaving approximately 10 feet between them. Using controls located on either side of the deck, the operator slides the carrier deck backwards toward the vehicle being towed. The deck angles down toward the street with the rear resting near the front tires of the inoperable vehicle. The carrier has a winch located in the center of the deck at the end closest to the truck's cab. A series of chains attached to the cable are released and hooked to the disabled vehicle's front axle or manufacturer-designed holes in the engine frame. Then it is merely a matter of winching the vehicle up onto the carrier's deck, leveling the deck, and shifting it back to the original position. After this is done, the operator attaches safety chains to the rear axle or engine frame slots on both sides of the vehicle to prevent any movement of the disabled vehicle.

Using a light-duty Ford Super Duty chassis and a carrier deck by Landoll, the tow operator provides special care for this Ferrari. This towing company provides service for a Ferrari dealer, towing the cars of high-profile athletes and wealthy business people who would rather not take the time to drive their expensive cars for regular maintenance, including oil changes. The towing company transports these beauties to the shop and back. If you have to ask the cost of this luxury, you can't afford it!

There is another means of loading these units. If a vehicle needs to be recovered from a precarious place, this will often be done with a heavy wrecker or crane. In these situations, since the vehicle is already suspended in the air, the flatbed can simply back under the wreck and allow the crane to lower the vehicle into place. Then the tow operator must secure the wreckage with chains.

Unloading the car is done in the reverse order from loading it. The difference is that as the bed is angled toward the ground, the car's weight and gravity are waiting to slide it backwards. The winch cable now acts as a means to control the speed of descent. As the operator slowly lets the cable out, the car rolls down until it stops on the level ground. If the tires are flat or the vehicle is wrecked,

This beautiful carrier was built primarily to haul forklifts. The truck has an overall length of 43 feet and a 30-foot bed that can accommodate eight forklifts being transported for service, rentals, or sales. The tri-axle chassis is a 1998 Freightliner Classic with a 500-horsepower Detroit 60 Series engine and a 13-speed Fuller transmission. The steel bed is by Chevron.

some tow operators will use liquid soap to make the bed slippery. Another trick is to unwind enough cable, wrap the cable around a stationary object behind the car for leverage, then attach the cable to the rear of the car. This allows the winch to pull the car off the truck's bed.

Since most automobile and light-duty truck manufacturers specify that certain vehicle models not be towed using sling-type equipment, wheel-lifts and carriers are used quite often. This is especially true with regard to certain drive systems, aerodynamic spoilers, lighter-gauge bumpers, and sheet metal on many cars. Any low profile sports car design will need a car carrier for damage-free towing.

Standard carriers have deck capacities ranging from 8,000 to 10,000 pounds and winch capacities that match. The length of the decks starts around 17 feet and can extend to 20 feet.

Heavy-duty carriers will have load capacities of 20,000 to 30,000 pounds. The higher-capacity units require tandem axles and a GVW of at least 50,000 pounds. These extra heavy units can feature decks up to 30 feet long. Some will even have an additional deck that sits above the truck's cab, enabling it to transport four vehicles simultaneously. One vehicle will be on the roof, two units on the extra-long deck, and a fourth unit in the wheel-lift at the rear.

Almost any kind of conventional light- or medium-duty truck chassis can be found sporting a carrier, although the trend today is away from the light-duty Class III & IV 10,000- to 16,000-pound GVW chassis. The Class V-VII

A flatbed built by Kilar on an IHC 4900 chassis is used to haul away the remains of a truck cab that was completely torn off the chassis in a terrible multivehicle accident on Interstate 55 near downtown Chicago. The Illinois Department of Transportation (IDOT) relocated the wrecks off the highway to local city streets where a private towing company completed the task.

When it snows, towing companies get extremely busy. This motorist turned too quickly and lost control of his car, ending up with the front end on top of a large, decorative rock. The tow operator was able to slide his flatbed under the rear end of the car and lift it to a position level with the front end. Then it was a simple matter of sliding the bed completely under the car to remove it from the rock.

18,000- to 35,000-pound GVW IHC 4000 series, Freightliner Business Class series, GMC/Chevy C series, and the Ford F series medium chassis seem to be more popular.

Many tow operators have found that the limits to what they can carry, both on the deck and with the wheel-lift, are determined by the original design and power of the chosen chassis. The more a tow operator wants to be able to carry, the bigger the GVW class of chassis that he needs to purchase. Power plants in these chassis range up to 400 horsepower.

Some tow companies specialize in towing very expensive cars like Porsches, Ferraris,

Lamborghinis, Rolls Royces, and Bentleys. These companies are very content to carry one car at a time. Often these operators will use Class III & IV chassis with a smaller GVW and cabs like the Ford Super Duty.

Some companies that manufacture carriers are Jerr-Dan, Champion, Century, AATAC, Chevron, Holmes, Dynamic, Kilar, and Challenger. These units seem very similar to the eye since there are no fabricated bodies constructed with compartments for tools or supplies. Each carrier is a truck chassis with a deck and perhaps a tool box. Subtle differences exist in hand rails or the edges of the decks, the shape of the cab protector, and steel versus aluminum decks. But from a distance, they appear very similar.

Carrier Changes

Due to the physical changes in modern vehicles, carrier designs have had to change as well to accommodate them. Since the number of vehicles with lower ground clearance has grown significantly in recent years, tow operators have experienced more and more difficulties in loading these vehicles. The trend among manufacturers to mount carriers upon heavier chassis, which sit higher off the

A close-up of a standard carrier using wooden planks to minimize the angle at the rear of the deck for this car with very little ground clearance.

ground compounds the problem, as well. The angle of the deck resting in front of the car to be towed is too steep to winch the car without risking damage. Tow drivers compensate for this by using metal ramps or wooden planks to reduce the angle of the deck. Heavy boards are placed in front of the tires to guide the cars onto the deck.

In response to this common situation, several companies have introduced new carrier designs with the purpose of eliminating ramps and planks by creating a deck that will meet the cars low on the street. The first such introduction is called The Right Approach by Century. This unit "allows the operator to lower the approach angle to 6 degrees, making the use of ramps or wood planks obsolete," according to company literature. The tip section of the deck is hinged to the balance of the deck, allowing it to be lowered almost flat on the ground while the remaining portion of the deck is angled in the normal fashion. Once the vehicle with the low clearance is on this tip section, it is raised until the entire deck is level. Now the car is winched fully onto the deck and it is loaded normally from this point.

A second design to load vehicles with low ground clearance is called the Stingray by Jerr-Dan. This unit has a solid one-piece deck, but they have changed the angle at the rear of the bed. Where conventional carriers

Here is an example of bulk transportation. When many cars need to be transported, this unit utilizes a nine-foot deck over the cab of the truck, a wheel-lift, and an extra-long 27-foot deck making it capable of carrying up to four vehicles. These wrecks are on their way to a regional insurance salvage yard. There is probably not much left of the two closest to the front.

A flatbed can come in very handy at an accident scene with two damaged vehicles. Instead of requiring a second truck, this driver first loaded one wreck onto the carrier deck. Then he simply backed up to the other car and locked it into the wheel-lift. An IHC 4900 medium-duty chassis serves as the base for this Challenger unit.

angle down at the tip, this unit is raised up. When the bed is angled to the ground, the tip now rests flat. This provides a low angle for the car to come onto the carrier deck.

The Job

As with light-duty tow trucks, when a carrier arrives on an accident scene, the driver is responsible for cleaning up the loose debris and spreading some sand on fluids that have leaked. Often there will be areas attached to the frame rails to carry five-gallon plastic pails either full of sand or empty to remove debris.

One carrier can do the work of two light-duty tow trucks and can increase an operator's profitability when there are two cars to pick up or deliver to the same place. At an accident scene, an operator can first load one car onto the deck and then load another car into the wheel-lift. For the same basic cost to the tow operator, two cars are carried without a second truck or driver.

From time to time, an operator will place a carrier on a chassis with an extended cab featuring four doors and a back seat. Although this lengthens the overall size, the benefits far outweigh any disadvantages. When picking up a vehicle that is disabled or was involved in an accident, the tow truck driver will often transport the driver with the vehicle, since no one can ride inside a vehicle being towed.

When a group of people or a family is involved, additional seating is required. These larger cabs go a long way to accommodate passengers who would otherwise need to make their own arrangements for transportation. In some cases with additional seating, the entire family can be driven home (which may include going to a neighboring state). While paying a higher towing bill, the car owner saves on hotel, rental car, and other out-of-town expenses.

In the event of a highway accident, the police will not leave people on the roadway. The officer will either transport the people or arrange for a cab to pick them up, staying

An example of a carrier with four doors and additional seating capacity. Pictured is a 1996 IHC 4700 with a DT466E Cummins engine and a 22-foot steel deck by Century.

A fter the fire department finished cutting this car apart to remove the injured driver and passenger, a flatbed came to remove the wreck. Just like postal workers, tow truck drivers must perform under all types of weather conditions.

with them until the cab arrives. This ties up the police officer unnecessarily. The ability of the tow operator to transport all of the passengers from the roadway goes a long way toward winning the favor of the police.

Lowboys

Another type of carrier is called a lowboy. Lowboys are not used for car transportation like flatbeds. Lowboys are trailers, approximately 40 feet long, that are pulled by a conventional over-the-road truck tractor. They are similar to trailers used by construction companies to move their heavy equipment between job sites.

Lowboys usually carry large loads, which cannot travel separately or be towed behind a wrecker. Loads that are extrawide, extralong, or do not have intact wheels will ride on a lowboy. Towing stretch limousines often requires a lowboy due to the car's length. The frame of a lowboy is set low to the ground,

A lowboy is used to carry this tank truck, which does not conform to truck restrictions and is not able to drive on public roads.

which allows it to carry big trucks without concern for overhead clearances.

A lowboy is loaded using a hydraulic system similar to that of a carrier. Using controls on the side of the frame, the operator slides the deck to the rear and raises the front-end, allowing a vehicle to drive right up the deck. The lowboy also has a winch to pull disabled vehicles onto the deck.

Lowboys differ from construction carriers in several ways. In order to load a construction carrier, the tractor is disconnected and the front end of the frame is lowered to the ground. A lowboy works from the rear and remains connected to the tractor. In addition, construction carriers are even lower to the ground than lowboys, allowing for bigger machinery to be transported. And construction carriers are able to transport heavier loads than lowboys. Although both offer models with different payload capacities, the construction units are generally able to carry more.

•FIVE•

Recoveries

The towing of disabled vehicles is but one aspect of the towing business. An area that is often larger, more complex, and more profitable to the towing and heavy wrecker companies involves recovery work. This encompasses accidents and other mishaps.

Although not all recovery work involves truck wrecks, the majority does. When a truck ends up on its side or upside down, loses its load, is torn apart, or just about anything else that cannot be handled by simply hooking it up, recovery work is involved. Usually the call to perform recovery work is received through contracts with trucking companies or through the police agencies that supervise various roads.

Many recoveries are fairly routine for the experienced operators, but often, the unexpected occurs. Trucks get stuck under

When the driver of this car fell asleep at the wheel, he traveled about 250 feet off the road. On his way, he hit trees on either side of the car, rolled over, and stopped when he hit a tree head-on. Instead of winching the car through the trees, Tauber's recovery team had access to grab the car with this impressive heavy wrecker and bring it back out to the street. The truck has a 1991 International 9400 chassis with a 400 Cummins engine and a 15-speed Fuller transmission. The body and boom are a 1996 30-ton Century 5030.

All four people aboard a private jet were killed when it crashed just 20 yards from a multi-family apartment building. After the Federal Aviation Administration (FAA) and National Transportation Safety Board (NTSB) personnel were ready to clear the scene, a towing company brought in several units. The bulk of the work was done with a unique 1991 Oshkosh six-wheel drive, tri-axle, 70-ton All Pro rotator to lift the debris and set it on a series of lowboys for the trip to an airport hanger.

Once the trailer section in this accident was winched up the embankment and held in place with this wrecker, another unit pulled the tractor section onto the slippery roadway.

viaducts, bridges, or in the mud. Loads shift, throwing trucks onto their sides. Slippery roads cause trucks to jackknife, and accidents can cause almost anything. Winching, lifting, righting, and securing are just some of the operations performed daily by recovery crews on and off roads around the country.

Specialized training and equipment are required during recoveries to ensure safety and to provide the best service possible to whomever is paying the bills. Schools are available to teach operators how to perform many recoveries safely. But just as frequently, the lessons are taught through hands-on experience by a family member in the business.

Anyone can enter the heavy-duty towing and recovery business simply by purchasing one of the big rigs and demanding a place on police rotation lists. Although this does not assure them access to recovery work, some companies have used just such steps to enter the highly specialized arena of truck accidents and recoveries.

Without the proper training and seasoning, though, this lack of experience can have devastating results. Consider, for instance, an untrained operator arriving at an accident scene on a busy highway and not placing his wrecker properly. This can result in a dangerous work area and cause a secondary accident. A secondary accident is one that results from traffic or unsafe conditions around an accident that is being cleared. There are some very frightening national statistics revealing the severity of injury and loss of life resulting from secondary accidents. Questions arise concerning who bears the responsibility for secondary accidents. The wrecker company, the highway department, or the police agency may be responsible.

The charred cab section of a car carrier is pulled onto the roadway by a homemade wrecker and a Hough front-end loader. A track excavator is visible in the background to help out.

Hazardous Materials Recovery

Not all recovery work is conventional. Sometimes recovery teams have to do whatever is necessary to get the job done.

One evening on Interstate 94 near Michigan City, Indiana, trucks were running in the right lane very slowly approaching the scales. Since there was a backup, trucks were crawling with their hazard lights flashing. Apparently, a fully loaded car carrier failed to notice the slow traffic and slammed into the rear of a tanker carrying a hazardous acid. The car carrier burst into flames, left the roadway, and rolled onto its side in the ditch. Sadly, the driver perished, leaving a nasty

scene that shut down the entire eastbound side of the interstate for 10 hours.

In this situation, the wrecker/recovery company stood by until the fire department, with its hazardous materials team, extinguished the fire, extricated the driver, and neutralized the area from the highly corrosive acid. Only then was the recovery team allowed to proceed. Each member working this particular recovery needed special protective suits, boots, and gloves in order to gain access to the wreck.

Equipment used during this four-hour recovery included a 1968 Auto Car Constructor, 1978 Hendrickson, and a 1974

One end of the car carrier is being lifted with a homemade heavy wrecker on a 1968 Autocar Constructor chassis. The Hough front-end loader is pulling the front of the car carrier to line it up with the wrecker.

Two heavy wreckers with homemade recovery bodies and mechanical booms are used to pull the charred car carrier. One unit has a 1974 Oshkosh 4x4 chassis and the other has a 1978 Hendrickson.

With one wheel off the ground, the Hough front-end loader keeps the rear of the car carrier high enough for the lowboy to be positioned underneath.

Oshkosh 4x4, all with nonhydraulic home-made booms and bodies. Additionally, a Hough front-end loader, a track excavator, and a lowboy were used.

After releasing the rear section of the loaded car carrier, which did not burn, came the difficult task of righting and winching the charred tractor section with three cars still on the carrier. The fourth car, which sat above the truck's cab, had been thrown clear and burned completely. The track excavator was used to go deep into the ravine to retrieve the loose car and add a little push as the truck was winched up the hill. Since the truck's tires were burned completely off, the winches had to pull the unit on its metal wheel rims after it was turned upright.

The combination of two wrecker winches and the Hough front-end loader dragged the charred truck up onto the roadway. Once on the roadway, it was dragged until it rested squarely in one lane. Then one end was lifted with the front-end loader and the other end with one of the wreckers. While the

The diver descends into the river to search for the submerged truck.

wrecked truck was suspended in the air, the lowboy was backed under it. Slowly the truck was lowered onto the lowboy and secured for its journey to the salvage yard.

The format for any recovery depends on what equipment the recovery team has at its disposal. For sure, though, any company wanting to be involved with heavy recovery work must have sufficient equipment to handle the unexpected wrecks that are becoming all too common on today's highways.

Water Recovery

Occasionally a towing company will be called upon to make an unusual recovery. Such is the case when a vehicle ends up under water. This type of recovery requires the assistance of an underwater diving company or the fire department to handle the work in the water.

One such accident involved a 12-ton tandem-axle dump truck, which rolled backwards down an embankment into a river after it was parked too close to the edge. Since no one saw the accident or knew for sure where the truck was, the first chore was for the diver to actually locate the truck and determine its position and condition. He reported that the red truck was submerged in roughly 15 feet of water approximately 30 yards offshore. The truck was upright and the wheels were almost totally buried in mud. Unlike a scuba diver, this diver used an air line hooked to a compressor on shore and was able to communicate clearly with his partner through a radio in his diving helmet.

Once the truck was located, the towing company winched out the cables for the diver to attach to the truck's axle with chains. It was important to use a cable looped through a snatch block to protect the winch motor and to guard against undue stress on the cable in this type of recovery.

The truck begins to appear as it is winched up from the river's bottom. *Dorothy Shapiro*

(The only limit to this configuration is the distance between the wrecker and the item being recovered. There has to be sufficient cable on the drum of the winch to allow the doubling.) After the cables were secured to the truck, the winching could begin. The red truck became visible through the dark green water. It emerged slowly and was winched to shore.

Due to the steep incline of the riverbank, the first wrecker, a 1981 Peterbilt tri-axle with a 60-ton hydraulic boom, needed to be close to the edge for pulling. But it was then unable to finish the job since there was no room to clear the embankment and bring the

A second wrecker is attached to the truck to hold it in place while the first wrecker (the tri-axle) is moved forward, allowing ample space for the dump truck to be pulled onto level ground. Note that each of the cables pulling the truck is doubled through a snatch block for added power and safety.

truck onto level ground. A second wrecker, a 1980 Kenworth C500 with a 50-ton Century hydraulic boom, was brought in to pull the truck farther up the embankment. After securing the dump truck with the second wrecker, the first wrecker was repositioned to assist with the final pull onto dry land.

The recovery itself was only the beginning of the truck owner's concerns. Externally, the truck looked pretty normal. However, inside the cab, snails and mollusks covered everything. The engine had to be taken completely apart and cleaned before the truck would be operational.

Once the tri-axle unit has moved sufficiently inland and is ready to winch the truck, the second wrecker will be disconnected so the dump truck can be pulled fully onto dry land.

The wrecker crew is attaching heavy recovery straps to the rear of the trailer, which will be supported by a 50-ton wrecker.

A loaded tractor-trailer swerved to avoid a reckless motorist and ended up on the center retaining wall. With wreckers attached at the front and rear of the wreck, air bags are inserted to lift the trailer. The recovery crew works closely together to ensure a safe recovery.

Air-Bag Recovery

When a tractor-trailer combination lands on its side, the big question before the truck is turned upright is whether the truck is empty or full. Righting an empty truck is a basic operation for any towing company. It becomes more tricky when righting trucks that are loaded. In this case, the wrecker company has two options.

The first option involves off-loading the cargo. This requires laborers and equipment in sufficient numbers to transfer the truck's contents into another truck. If the cargo is intact and accessible, the truck's owners can have the freight reloaded to continue the delivery. If the truck is demolished, off-loading becomes a must. Afterwards, the wrecker crew has an empty rig to turn upright.

If the cargo is not accessible to off-load and the trailer is unbroken, or if the cargo and trailer are relatively intact, then the towing company has a second option, to right the trailer with the full load in place. This means less time at the accident scene and, therefore, a shorter time for lane closures and blockage. Depending on the weight of the contents and the material construction of the trailer, it may be possible to turn the load

While the driver was out of the truck, his tractor and dump trailer rolled backwards and down 100 feet into a quarry. Two heavy wreckers were used to pull the unit back up the hill. A 1978 Challenger 8800 50-ton hydraulic wrecker on a Peterbilt chassis with a Detroit Diesel engine was supplemented by a Challenger CH45 on a 1986 IHC F9370 chassis with a Cummins engine. The loose dirt forming the side of the quarry greatly increased the load while the dump trailer was pulled up the hill.

upright with wreckers using straps and cables. If this is not possible or safe, then towing and recovery teams use inflatable air bags, also referred to as air cushions.

Since trailers are built with the premise that they will stay on their wheels, the load bearing platform, or strength, is in the floor. Sides in an aluminum trailer are very thin compared to the steel-reinforced wooden floors. If a wrecker were to attempt to right a loaded trailer without air bags, the heavy load might tear right through the truck's sides as it is being lifted. This would drop the load onto the street, ruining both the load and the truck.

Air bags are made of thick polyester and vinyl, or urethane. They are inserted flat under the side of the trailer, and can lift up to 23,000 pounds. Using a controller unit to regulate the air going into each bag, air is then pumped in with a compressor. As the bags inflate, they put pressure on the sides of the truck to keep the load from pushing through. The air bags alone usually lift the truck.

Depending on the size and weight involved, from one to three wreckers will be used to assist with the lift and secure the load in case of a malfunction or other unforeseen mishap. Using straps, winches, and the booms, the wreckers will work in tandem with the bags to slowly right the truck and trailer. The

In addition to the soft dirt forming the sides of the quarry, the loose footing of the delicate soil underneath the wreckers required the use of four cables to complete the pull and drag the trailer onto level ground. Once on solid ground, the trailer was righted and towed away.

wreckers will then ensure that the truck comes to rest gently on its wheels in a controlled manner. Otherwise, the truck would simply drop hard and risk tipping to the other side. Air-bag recovery is a highly skilled operation and requires precise control coordinated between all of the workers involved.

If done properly, a truck righted with air bags can be safely unloaded at a location well off the road. The cargo can then be transferred with no further damage, and the new truck can be on its way.

Emergency Extrication

Fire department rescue squads are responsible for extricating, or freeing, trapped victims in the event of a traffic accident. They carry specialized tools for cutting,

A special strap wraps around the bus and attaches to the dual cables on the hydraulic boom. A twin unit stands by with a cable acting as a safety on the front of the bus. Both units have Century wrecker bodies and booms.

Photos illustrate Jim's Towing of Bensenville, Illinois, working with area fire departments and other officials at a mock disaster involving a loaded school bus that was struck by a train. The scenario involved the possibility that a victim or victims were trapped underneath the bus. Two Century 30-ton units with integrated hydraulic booms and under-lifts on Kenworth T800 chassis were used to lift the bus off the ground, allowing the fire department to inspect underneath.

prying, and forcing apart just about any-thing that can trap someone.

Fire department rescue squads also have air bags for rescue situations. But these differ from those carried by towing companies. Fire department air bags can only lift a relatively small distance off the ground, whereas recovery air bags can inflate to eight feet.

The ability to lift an entire wreck to free a trapped victim has become more prevalent in the United States in recent years. In Europe, many fire departments have cranes or wrecker-like-lifts to accomplish this task. Several fire departments in the United States have also incorporated this technology, although their lifting capacity is usually no more than 16,000 pounds. Since the majority do not have these capabilities within their own departments, they have started to rely on the expertise of wrecker operators to assist them. Previously, the wrecker operator would not have been used until the scene was secured by the fire department. Now, wrecker operators are becoming integral on-scene resources.

Such was the case when a tractor-trailer landed completely on its roof, trapping the driver on a highway in Illinois. The wrecker crew was on the scene for several hours while the fire department was attempting to free the driver. His leg was badly pinned, and a doctor was called to the scene and asked about amputating it. When the doctor said that this was not an option, the fire chief looked to the wrecker operator for assistance. Two wreckers were put into action. They lifted the truck, allowing the driver to be removed.

After this incident, area fire departments began talking to local towing and recovery companies to begin coordinating their efforts. This would permit heavy equipment and skilled operators to be available for assistance when their specialized services could save lives. Many tow operators have been involved in helping to save lives when the fire department was unable to do so.

Education, communication, and awareness are the keys to making this joint effort successful.

Load Recovery

When an accident occurs involving loaded trucks, sometimes the truck is badly damaged, requiring the cargo to be removed. In other accidents, severe damage to the trucks causes their cargo to spill onto the roadway or shoulder areas. In either case, someone has to move, transfer, or recover the load, whether it is machine parts, livestock, garbage, or any other commodity that travels by truck. The towing and recovery company will be more than happy to supply the equipment and labor to undertake this job–for a fee.

Since the towing company is working for the truck's owner, they will do their best to off-load or salvage the product without any further damage in order to minimize the loss. This is accomplished with cranes, end loaders, forklifts, and good old-fashioned elbow grease. In the case of small or fragile merchandise, a recovery team assembly line is usually the method of choice. If the load is down a hill or in a ditch, perhaps many back-breaking trips up to the roadway is the only way to get the job done. When the load is unsanitary, end loaders usually handle the work. In foul or

Cleaning up the debris scattered around the roadway after a loaded trailer was torn open is the responsibility of the wrecker/recovery team. At this scene, a front-end loader is used to scoop the cargo onto a flatbed trailer.

good weather, the job still needs to be completed efficiently and safely.

Conflicts can arise when accidents occur on private tollways, turnpikes, bridges, and tunnels. Here, the incident commander representing the roadway wants to expedite the recovery and salvage to minimize the lane closures and inconvenience to motorists. The recovery company is bound to work within the guidelines set forth by the road authority and to follow the instructions of the incident commander.

This was the case when a load of lawn mower engines and other parts was strewn all over a highway when the trailer they were in was torn open in an accident with another truck. In an effort to open the highway, the incident commander from the road authority called for two highway department front-end loaders. They pushed the load off the highway onto the shoulder and then aided the recovery company by scooping up the debris and dumping it into a stake-bed semitruck. When inspected by the insurance company,

After the rear section and axle of this trailer were severed in an accident, two front-end loaders were used to lift it while a lowboy was placed underneath. As the end loaders supported the trailer, members of the recovery team used a torch to cut off the trailer's supporting legs so it could lie flat on the lowboy.

the load was determined to be a total loss exceeding $100,000. Had the load been recovered by hand, the towing company estimated only a 10 percent loss.

Tank Truck Recovery

Everyone sees those big tankers barreling down the highways. The contents of some are clearly marked, while others can be determined from the company name dis-played on the side of the trailer. Although every truck has placards or signs which classify the product being carried, most motorists have no idea whether they are driving next to milk, corn syrup, petroleum products, or highly corrosive and toxic chemicals.

When an accident occurs, it can be a motorist's worst nightmare. Stories fill the news weekly about precautionary evacuations, road closures, and long traffic delays due to overturned tank trucks carrying dangerous products.

There are several common causes for these mishaps. Driver fatigue is one. Unsafe or erratic driving by someone in a car interfering with the truck is another. Speed on the part of the truck driver is a third. Last, liquid products are very heavy and can shift during turns and other maneuvers causing the truck to be unstable and hard to control. More and more, unstable loads are causing spills and accidents on highway exit and entrance ramps.

When a tanker turns over, the tank is not always ruptured. Sometimes it lands intact.

In this case, an experienced wrecker operator will be able to right the truck fully loaded. The odds are in his favor that the unit will remain intact.

The question that always arises is "What if?" What if the tank is unstable and ruptures during the lift, spilling the load? Who is responsible for the added cleanup costs? The answers are not always apparent. Each situation is unique.

Factors involved include the location, road blockage, proximity to a water supply that could be contaminated, and of course, the degree of danger posed by the product. If the tank is ruptured during the accident and

A rear view of the trailer that was ripped open shows the cargo inside. Workers are under the trailer with torches cutting off the support legs.

When a tanker loaded with 8,000 gallons of Ethanol lost control on a highway exit ramp, it flipped and skidded, rupturing the tank in several places. After an eight-hour containment effort and off-loading the hazardous product into another tank truck, the wrecker company was given the approval to finish the job. Using a construction-grade model 1500 National crane, along with a Century 9055 wrecker at the rear axle, the tanker was lifted with a sling and placed onto its wheels. The force of the impact was enough to tear the fifth wheel from the tractor which required the trailer and tractor to be towed separately.

product is spilled or leaking, the first step is containment. Off-loading the product to another tank truck is often the next step. This can take more than eight hours if the conditions are less than ideal.

Usually, it is only after the tanker has been off-loaded that the wreckers will be allowed to proceed. Turning the truck upright involves the use of special slings, which surround the tank and attach to the wrecker boom or crane. Cables attached to

the axles can also be a part of this recovery process. Sometimes the tank truck is lifted completely off the ground and then rotated upright before being lowered onto its wheels. Another technique is to lift the tank straight up while pulling with cables to right the unit without the wheels ever leaving the ground. Still a third method to be used, when the truck rests on a cement retaining wall, is to simply pivot the truck over the wall allowing it to rest on its wheels.

Many towing companies employ surplus military tow trucks to supplement their off-road capabilities. Actually, the military refer to these units as cranes. Here, a 1952 International M-62 6x6 15-ton rotator lifts a wreck by a creek. The boom can rotate 360 degrees and extend up to 18 feet. This particular truck has worked at many off-road recoveries, including several along the rail lines.

A tank truck that rolled over the cement retaining wall is brought back onto its wheels with a 70-ton rotator. Notice that traffic lanes are still open because the rotator allows the recovery team to work off the side of the wrecker.

Watching these massive trucks being put back on their wheels, no matter which method is used, is an incredible sight.

Trailer Uprighting

Truck trailers find themselves on their sides more often than one might think. Bringing them back upright is a common and basic technique for most wrecker operators. It is referred to as a "side-to-side controlled roll" using recovery straps, and the procedure is simple. Generally, two units are used. One acts as the controller and can be any size truck with a winch. The other unit does the lifting.

First off, three heavy recovery straps are placed around the body of the trailer. Using heavy steel "D" rings, two of the straps are attached to the cables of the main wrecker on one side of the rig. The third strap is attached to the cable of the controller unit on the opposite side of the overturned rig. As the heavy unit lifts, the second truck controls the rig, preventing it from bouncing or tipping over from its own weight when it is brought upright. Gently, the trailer is then lowered onto its wheels.

Recovery work combines the largest wreckers, with a great deal of teamwork and knowledge, to clean up the spills and accidents that occur on our nation's roadways.

Two heavy wreckers are used to right this trailer in a maneuver referred to as a "controlled roll." One unit is a 1995 International Eagle with a Detroit Series 60 470 engine, a 13-speed Fuller transmission, and a Century 1040SB-SDU 40-ton wrecker body. The other unit acting as a controller is a 1989 Kenworth W900 with a Cummins 444 engine, a 13-speed Fuller transmission, and a Century 1040-SDU back end. Interestingly, each unit has a single rear axle with an air-pusher axle for optimal weight distribution.

Repair Shop Recovery

The car is resting on its side between the hydraulic lifts.

With the car suspended from the boom, the wrecker is repositioned in order to set the car on its wheels.

While a mechanic at a suburban auto dealership was working on a customer's car, one of the steel support arms on the hydraulic lift broke loose, dropping the car approximately six feet onto its side.

The call went out to Rogner's Towing Company for help. They responded with two units. One was a 1968 Holmes #1701 35-ton hydraulic heavy-duty wrecker on a Kenworth T600 chassis powered by a 265-horsepower Cummins engine. (Rogner's is the proud owner of the second hydraulic wrecker ever made by Holmes. The first was used as a demonstrator and never sold to a towing company.) The second unit on this recovery was an aluminum flatbed by Chevron on an IHC 4600 chassis.

Working in very tight quarters, the recovery workers first secured the car with straps and then slowly picked it up, being careful not to let it sway into the shop's hydraulic lift, causing further damage. When the car was off the floor and suspended by the wrecker, it was repositioned into the middle of the shop and lined up directly behind the flatbed. After attaching two straps from the winch on the flatbed to the undercarriage of the car, the heavy wrecker slowly lowered the car while the straps on the flatbed were winched closer, literally pulling the bottom of the car level with the floor.

The car was set gently onto its wheels, in what appeared to be slow motion, and was then winched onto the flatbed for the journey to the body shop. The car sustained approximately $17,000 in damage from the fall, which was not further complicated due to the careful recovery. Although the car was not totaled by the insurance company, the customer decided not to keep it.

Pity the person who had to tell the customer when he came to claim his car!

Two straps are attached to a carrier, which serve to pull the bottom of the car level with the ground, while the heavy wrecker lowers the cables holding the car.

•SIX•
Government and Municipal Fleets

Many branches of the federal government, in addition to some local and state agencies, have fleets of trucks. Several of these agencies also maintain their own tow trucks. These vehicles, and the agencies that oversee them, are very specialized.

IDOT

In the late 1950s and early 1960s, the interstate highway system was developed, linking cities around the country. As populations grew, problems occurred on the highways approaching major cities during what is now known as "rush hour." In Illinois, state engineers and other employees were asked to drive these highways during peak travel times to determine why these new super-highways were not providing the traffic flow that they were designed for. When interviewed, the engineers reported that everything was satisfactory except for the occasional breakdown or accident that would end up blocking lanes of traffic, causing backups and delays. After witnessing

Three of IDOT's heavy wreckers are lined up and working to clear an accident that has shut down the entire highway in one direction.

This police department tow operator was surprised to look in his rear-view mirror and see that the car in his sling was on fire. All he could do was wait until the fire department arrived and hope that the fire would be extinguished without damage to his truck.

such backups for a period of time and being unable to help, several of these engineers and other employees decided to carry items in their cars to help the motorists who were causing these delays. Some began to carry jumper cables, a spare can of gas, and tire irons to provide motorist assistance. Later, these state employees realized that additional supplies would be of service to them, and they began to increase the amount of equipment they carried.

As time went on, the engineers and other employees were spending more time assisting motorists and less time working at their regular state jobs. It was decided to hire people specifically for the purpose of helping motorists during the peak traffic hours. Gradually, the amount and types of equipment that were carried grew as recommendations were made to provide greater assistance to motorists. This broadened into a full-time staff of patrollers whose sole function was to

With Chicago's fabulous skyline as a backdrop, a USPS VMF light-duty truck tows a disabled LDV. Translated, that means a 1988 Grumman light-duty delivery vehicle is towed by a vehicle maintenance facility tow truck for the United States Postal Service.

When a container truck struck a railroad overpass and flipped onto a car in the next lane, miraculously none of the car's occupants was hurt. Since the accident occurred on a bridge over the interstate and blocked an exit ramp, IDOT was summoned to clear the scene. IDOT's unit is a Century 60-ton rotator on a White-Volvo Autocar 6x6 chassis, powered by a 425-horsepower Caterpillar engine with an Allison deep reduction five-speed automatic transmission. IDOT raised the container with the help of a 50-ton 8800 Challenger heavy wrecker from the Chicago Transit Authority (CTA) fleet.

concentrate on keeping the traffic lanes open. They were assigned patrol vehicles which were upgraded to include chains for pulling cars off the road, large bumpers for pushing cars off the road, and later, welded pipe booms with winches to tow cars and trucks off the road.

Today, the Illinois Department of Transportation (IDOT) operates this unique service for the motoring public that uses the metro-Chicago interstate highway system. Although there are other state-run operations elsewhere, IDOT is known as the grandfather of state-sponsored highway assistance programs. The IDOT fleet currently consists of 51 units. IDOT patrols the highways 24 hours a day, offering free motorist assistance including jump starts, gasoline, relocation of disabled vehicles, accident removal, and heavy-duty recovery.

A total of 71 highway miles, representing 718 lane miles on seven different interstate expressways, is under the responsibility of the IDOT Emergency Traffic Patrol. Known locally as the *Minute Men* for their rapid response to traffic emergencies and disabled vehicles, this group handles over 100,000 incidents annually that affect highway safety and hamper traffic flow. Stalls in traffic are swiftly relocated to the shoulder or to one of the many paved areas located throughout the region, where accidents can be safely investigated. IDOT's area of operations also encompasses entrance ramps and any other areas that affect the smooth flow of traffic on these highways.

Although private towing companies also provide towing and roadside assistance on

When a small excavator toppled off a trailer and blocked a lane, two IDOT EPVs responded to the scene. While one EPV blocked traffic, the other unit righted the vehicle and cleared the lane.

One of the most frequently recurring recovery operations involves lifting and moving large rolls of steel that come free of their chains. This roll created a six-inch-deep crevice on interstate 90/94 in Chicago during one evening's rush-hour commute. The mishap caused the lane to be shut down overnight for emergency repairs. IDOT's 60-ton Century rotator on a White-Volvo Autocar chassis carried the steel off the highway, where a private company then removed it. One of IDOT's EPV medium-duty IHC trucks is in the background.

these highways, it is IDOT's responsibility to clear the traffic lanes of any obstructions before turning the vehicles over to the private companies. IDOT patrol units carry fire extinguishers and first aid supplies, because they often arrive at accident scenes before fire and emergency medical service (EMS) units. When fire and EMS units arrive, the *Minute Men* handle traffic duties to ensure everyone's safety. Once the state police and fire department personnel finish their tasks, IDOT clears the roadway.

The IDOT fleet consists of 35 Emergency Patrol Vehicles (EPVs) which are medium-duty trucks on IHC 4900 chassis with 210-horsepower DT466 TA engines, Allison automatic transmissions, and specially designed bodies with boom/wheel-lift assemblies by B & B Industries. Four heavy-duty recovery units on Autocar, Peterbilt, and International Paystar chassis with 60- and 50-ton rotators handle the big jobs. In addition, a sand spreader, a rescue truck with extrication equipment, a mobile command/support unit, and nine small 4x4s for the supervisors round out the fleet. The command/support unit is a 1992 Chevy step van with cots, a generator, lights, air cushions, self-contained breathing apparatus (SCBA), equipment to deal with hazardous materials, and medical supplies.

The original fleet of EPVs, which had consisted of mechanical welded pipe boom units, was replaced with 35 rather unique trucks. Each unit in the fleet is identical for standardization. The booms are hydraulic with 20,000-pound capacities, and the wheel-lifts can be completely controlled from inside the cab. In order to facilitate working without leaving the cab, the trucks have a sloped rear body section to provide the driver with increased visibility out of the rear window. This design was added to reduce the dangers to the drivers when finding stalled or abandoned vehicles in traffic. They no longer have to exit the vehicle with traffic on all sides traveling in excess of 70 miles per hour. The *Minute Man* simply places his truck in front of the stalled vehicle, lowers the wheel-lift, and backs up to the vehicle until the wheel-lift touches the wheels. Then the claws of the wheel-lift, which are set between the car's front tires, wrap around each tire and IDOT is ready to relocate the stalled car.

The drive line and frames of the EPVs are reinforced to allow them to relocate a loaded tractor trailer off the expressway. An engine-mounted compressor permits filling flat tires, releasing trailer air brakes, and inflating air bags for recovery work.

Unlike conventional wheel-lifts that protrude straight out to the rear of most tow trucks, IDOT's wheel-lift units are designed to fold up vertically along the boom assembly. This is intended to provide as flat a rear end as possible, hoping to minimize damage and injury to motorists who might strike the rear of an EPV at high speed.

Although IDOT sometimes works with private towing companies at an accident scene, IDOT's policies and priorities often differ from private towing and recovery companies when incidents involve trucks. Whereas a private company is working for the truck's owner and strives to provide damage-free towing and recovery, IDOT maintains responsibility to the motorists by trying to minimize lane blockage. Its chief concerns are to keep IDOT personnel safe and to maintain a safe environment for motorists, so IDOT will do whatever is necessary to clear the lanes in the shortest period of time. This may mean causing additional damage to the truck involved in the accident when the rig is dragged to a spot off the roadway. There the truck can be turned upright and recovered by a private company without disrupting the traffic flow and causing congestion.

To further enhance IDOT's capabilities to respond swiftly to any occurrence that ties up traffic, trucks will soon be equipped with vehicle location equipment using global positioning systems (GPS) to provide automated dispatching of the closest EPV.

U.S. Postal Service

The United States Postal Service (USPS) operates a massive nationwide active fleet of over 208,000 vehicles, including cars and small, medium, and large trucks. The largest category of vehicles are 1/2-ton trucks used by carriers to deliver the mail. These Light Delivery Vehicles (LDV) account for almost 145,000 units of the total vehicle inventory.

Every vehicle in this fleet is the responsibility of one of the Vehicle Maintenance Facilities (VMF). The country is divided into 85 districts with a total of 334 VMFs. In most areas, the USPS handles all truck maintenance and towing. In outlying areas, a vehicle might not see a VMF except once a year for preventative maintenance; similarly, routine maintenance and towing are contracted out to private companies where it is not cost-effective to handle these duties in-house. The balance of the fleet, though, will be towed, tuned, and fixed by the regional VMFs.

To keep the mail moving, the VMFs have their own fleet of tow trucks and wreckers. This fleet is very diverse, covering the spectrum of light-duty, medium-duty, and heavy-duty trucks. Consistent throughout, of course, is the familiar USPS color scheme and eagle logo. As the saying goes, "the mail must get through," and the Postal Service fleet is an integral part of ensuring an uninterrupted flow of letters and parcels.

In the tradition of government service, the USPS maintains a competitive bidding process to purchase equipment. Combining USPS requests with requests from other branches of the government, the General Services Administration (GSA) will seek out suppliers that satisfy the requirements for this equipment, and will award a purchase order to the lowest bidder.

The purchase of tow trucks follows this procedure. Over the years, this has meant several different configurations in the towing fleet. Since all ordering is done centrally in Washington, D.C., there is not a very diverse cross section of tow trucks throughout the country. Every vehicle in the fleet is purchased with an expected service life. For tow trucks this is 8 to 10 years. When there is a need for replacement in one of the VMFs and the purchase is made, the equipment is delivered to a regional center where it is accepted by the Postal Service. It is then sent to the district VMFs as needed to replace the aging equipment. Trucks that have been replaced are put up for auction as surplus equipment.

Trucks in the Postal Service fleet have been built by such manufacturers as No Mar, Holmes, Century, Jerr-Dan, Challenger, B & B Industries, and Canfield. Although the exact number of tow trucks nationally is not readily available, it is believed that there are between 500 and 600 units throughout the country.

In recent years, flatbeds and roll-backs have been added to the fleet of tow trucks with booms. These units increase the efficiency of transporting multiple vehicles long distances between facilities.

One of the most recent national contracts for Postal Service tow trucks was awarded in 1997 for 16 10-ton Jerr-Dan units with hydraulic booms and separate wheel-lifts. The chassis are from Chevrolet with 15,000 pound GVWs, although the next generation units will have specifications for heavier 17,500 pound GVW chassis.

The biggest heavy wrecker in the USPS fleet is stationed at the Chicago District. Affectionately nicknamed *Big Bertha*, this unit is a 1983 Holmes 850 dual-boom mechanical wrecker on a White-Volvo Autocar chassis.

Big Bertha, the giant heavy wrecker in the USPS Chicago District VMF, is a 1983 Holmes 850 on a big Autocar chassis. This unit is especially useful in the winter months. Here it is towing a tractor to the VMF.

In addition to this heavy wrecker, there are medium-duty trucks, which were purchased in 1996 with Century 820 units on Ford F800 chassis with 20-ton capacities.

Rounding out the tow truck fleet in the Chicago District are light-duty trucks purchased in 1994 with Century Model 612 wrecker bodies, which have 12-ton capacities. These trucks are on Ford Super Duty chassis, and are replacing units with bodies by Canfield on Dodge Power Wagon chassis, which are pending disposal as surplus.

The VMFs with the largest number of tow trucks are in Atlanta, Houston, and San Diego. They maintain fleets consisting of approximately 4,000 vehicles each. The Atlanta VMF, which is responsible for 4,400 total vehicles, has eight facilities with 15 tow trucks. The largest wrecker in their fleet is a rebuilt Holmes 750 purchased many years ago from the military. Originally on a Ford chassis, the unit was remounted on a Mack MC chassis with a 283-horsepower engine.

VMF towing operations involve accident recovery, disabled vehicles, and pickup of vehicles from outlying stations for routine

preventative maintenance or "PM." This permits the VMF to send one driver with a tow truck to bring in an LDV. Otherwise, they would either have to send two men to retrieve the unit or require the station to tie up a letter carrier to drive the unit to the shop. Since this would delay mail delivery, it is not an option. During the peak holiday season, the USPS requires around-the-clock manning of the tow trucks. Time is too critical to delay a response from the VMF.

Maryland Transportation Authority

The Maryland Transportation Authority (MDTA) is responsible for maintaining and operating four bridges, two tunnels, and 50 miles of Interstate 95, the John F. Kennedy Memorial Highway between Baltimore and Delaware. The MDTA, a private organization that relies solely on the collection of user fees or tolls for its revenue, provides road maintenance, police patrol, motorist assistance, and emergency services, which are supplemented by local agencies.

The four bridges are widely spread around the state. They include the Harry W. Nice Memorial Bridge in the south; the William Preston Lane Jr. Memorial Bridge (also known as the Chesapeake Bay Bridge) to the east; the Thomas J. Hatem Memorial Bridge crossing the Susquehanna River to the north; and the Francis Scott Key Bridge outside of Baltimore.

The Fort McHenry and Baltimore Harbor Tunnels are also in the metropolitan Baltimore area. Each tunnel is 1 1/2 miles in length with up to eight lanes for traffic. Over 20 million vehicles travel through the Baltimore Harbor Tunnel annually, while the Fort McHenry Tunnel handles over 37 million. The tunnels also include 20 miles of ramps and approach roads.

Assisting motorists around the clock, responding to vehicle fires, and clearing car and truck accidents in order to keep the lanes of traffic open are the responsibilities of the Vehicle Recovery Technicians (VRTs). VRTs are stationed during peak travel times of the summer and holidays at the Bay Bridge, and around the clock at the Nice Bridge and in the central region, which includes the tunnels and the Key Bridge. Duties at the Hatem bridge are handled by the police, who are equipped with Jeeps.

Cargo that is considered to be hazardous is not permitted in the tunnels. Any vehicle carrying hazardous materials is required to use the Key Bridge. Violating this requirement brings very stiff fines.

The VRTs have a fleet of 11 trucks. Five of the trucks are conventional light-duty tow trucks on Ford Super Duty chassis with Chevron bodies. Others have the outward appearance of miniature heavy wreckers. These units are custom-made to perform their duties. The two newest trucks are built on 1996 Mack MR chassis with 300-horsepower Mack engines, nine-speed Mack air-shift automatic transmissions, and towing bodies and booms by Weld-Built. They have a very short 97-inch wheelbase to allow a three-point turn in the narrow confines of a

The Maryland Transportation Authority (MDTA) purchased two of these specialized units to work in the tunnels outside of Baltimore. Built on a Mack MR chassis, the truck has an extra-short wheel base that permits tight turns in the narrow tunnels.

The MDTA has four units like this short Freightliner COE with a Weld-Built body. Two will be placed into reserve status when the newer Mack units reach front-line service.

tunnel or bridge. They are equipped with first-aid supplies and conventional towing gear. Also in the fleet are three 1984 units on 112-inch wheelbase Freightliner COE chassis with Weld-Built bodies. One other similar unit has an International chassis. The older units have dual mechanical booms with 16-ton capacities while the newer units have fixed hydraulic booms capable of lifting 20 tons. Each heavy unit also has an 8,000-pound front winch.

The Freightliner units were designed with hose reels and 300-gallon water tanks for vehicle fires. Additional equipment previously included protective clothing for fighting fires. The Mack units no longer have fire fighting equipment.

The VRTs in the past went through rigorous training as fire fighters, as medical first responders, and as towing and recovery equipment operators before working for the MDTA. Changing times and liability concerns have added hazardous materials training but removed the fire and medical duties. In the event of an accident, basic attempts to stop bleeding are about the extent of the medical treatment that a VRT is allowed to perform while waiting for an ambulance to arrive from local or city medic units under contract with the MDTA. Likewise, VRTs have fire extinguishers to attack vehicle fires until backup personnel responding from surrounding fire departments arrive.

Working eight-hour shifts, the central region crew handles both tunnels from three emergency stations. Two garages flank the Fort McHenry Tunnel, while the third is at the Harbor Tunnel. They handle roughly 6 to 12 calls per shift for breakdowns and minor accidents. Although major accidents and incidents involving trucks are not frequent, approximately 50 occur each year.

The VRTs will also respond to approximately 13 miles of Interstate 95 to clear the traffic lanes of wrecks and stalls. After the VRTs have relocated the vehicles to the shoulder, a private towing company will take over.

Boston Tunnel Authority

Around the city of Boston, there are three tunnels that allow commuters to travel under the Boston Harbor. The Sumner Tunnel, the Callahan Tunnel, and the newer Ted Williams Tunnel are all intended to permit uninterrupted traffic flow. As anyone who travels through these tunnels knows, this is not always the case. The Sumner and Callahan Tunnels are side by side, with lengths of nine-tenths of a mile. The Williams Tunnel, which opened in December of 1995, is a mile and a half.

The tunnels and the turnpikes are under the authority of MASSPIKE, the Massachusetts Turnpike Authority; so is the newest project referred to as *The Big Dig* or the Central Artery. This new tunnel project, which is scheduled to reach completion in the year 2006, is being dug directly under the entire city of Boston. Among the usual dangers and difficulties, building this tunnel requires boring between two rail tunnels that are already in place.

Although the Ted Williams Tunnel is much more spacious than the older tunnels, it does not take much to bring traffic to a crawl or a complete halt. In an effort to ensure a minimum of disruption when accidents, stalls, or breakdowns occur,

above and right:

One of the units operated by MASSPIKE hooks a stranded car in the Ted Williams Tunnel in Boston. The capability to tow a car from wheel-lifts located at the front and rear of the tow truck allows the operator to approach a stall from either direction. Both hookups are shown here.

MASSPIKE operates the Emergency Response System (ERS), which is responsible for aiding motorists and removing vehicles that upset the normal traffic flow. The ERS buildings are staffed around the clock by Instant Response Operators (IROs) who are stationed in buildings at each end of the tunnels. The IROs man a fleet of six tow trucks and various other support equipment. Flat tires, tows, stalls, and wrecks are handled by the IROs, who remove vehicles from the tunnels and relocate them to a safe place outside.

The fleet consists of two medium-duty trucks on Ford F800 chassis and four light-duty trucks on Ford Super Duty chassis. The light-duty units are virtually identical. Two were purchased in 1995 and the other two in 1993. They are equipped with wheel-lifts on both the front and rear of each unit that can be operated by interior controls. This unique setup was put in place to handle situations that occur in the narrow tunnels, whether the IRO approaches from behind or in front of the disabled vehicle. Congestion created by an incident may mean that the IRO will have to enter the tunnel against traffic. Having a wheel-lift on the front of the truck allows swift pick-up of the vehicle. A simple breakdown presents very real danger to the IRO when traffic is able to move in the next lane. If the wheel-lift controls were in the conventional place at the rear of the truck, the IRO would be in a vulnerable position while hooking up the car. The interior controls allow the IRO to work from the safety of the truck's cab. This is not only safer, but it is also extremely efficient.

Chicago Transit Authority

The Chicago Transit Authority (CTA) operates buses and rapid transit trains throughout the city of Chicago and into many surrounding suburbs. The fleet consists of almost 2,000 large transit buses, an assortment of other vehicles, and more than 1,100 rapid transit train cars. In order to keep everything moving, the CTA has 7 main garages around the city for storage and maintenance of vehicles, in addition to 11 rail yards for the trains.

The CTA operates eight heavy wreckers, four of which are manned around the clock. Three units are kept as spares and the biggest rig is ready for action at any time. These units are specially equipped to tow buses and assist with getting rail cars back on the tracks. The largest of these units is on

Another CTA wrecker tows a transit bus. This unit is a 1989 White GMC Autocar with a Challenger 8800 hydraulic wrecker. It is utilizing an under-lift since this bus has very low ground clearance.

a 1989 White-Volvo Autocar chassis with a 50-ton 8800 wrecker body by Challenger. The other trucks are extremely specialized. These units feature Autocar or Ford Louisville chassis, and custom bodies, booms, and elevating platforms. Each truck carries an assortment of equipment including chains, axes, hand-jacks, and other items to get rail cars back on the track if they derail. Most feature Detroit Series 60 engines, tubular-framed mechanical booms, and elevating towers that can reach three stories high.

Chicago is known for the elevated rail system, or the "El," which encircles the downtown financial district. The wreckers

with elevating platforms are designed to assist with evacuations from the overhead tracks should an accident or disabled train require removal of the passengers. Painted red and equipped with emergency lights and sirens, these units handle much more than the average breakdown. Accidents involving CTA vehicles, and all rail incidents in the metro area, initiate a response from at least one of these special trucks. Any type of accident that disrupts CTA service will also receive a wrecker. The CTA will clear car wrecks and other debris to ensure uninterrupted public transportation. Since these trucks are larger than the city tow trucks and manned around the clock, the CTA drivers are frequently called to assist the Chicago police and fire departments with accidents and breakdowns. Also at their disposal are air bags and a host of other extrication equipment. Any incidents where trains or buses come into contact with people or vehicles are handled by these emergency personnel and their vehicles.

IDOT, the Maryland Transportation Authority, the Boston Tunnel Authority, and the Chicago Transit Authority are specialized agencies created to meet the demands of transportation in America. With the help of tow trucks, whether they are light-duty, medium-duty, heavy-duty, or flatbeds, these agencies and private towing companies across the United States help keep the motoring public, trains, buses, and trucks on the move.

The Chicago Transit Authority (CTA) operates this 1992 White GMC Autocar with body, platform, and towing equipment supplied by several companies. Here it is towing a disabled bus with a Holmes-hitch fabricated for this style of bus.

INDEX